C000135116

IMAGES
of England

WINSFORD

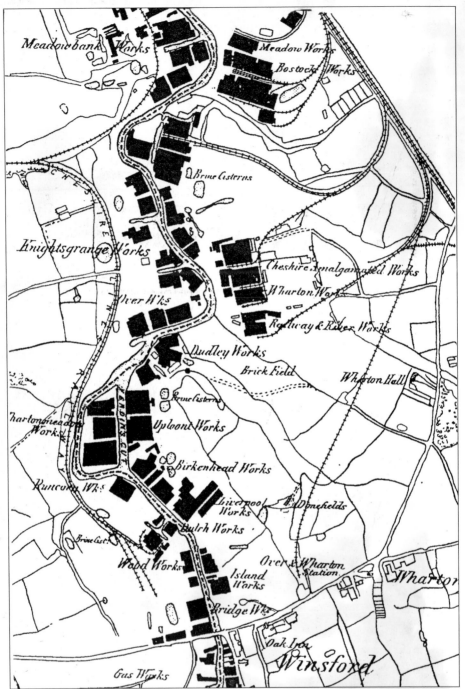

By 1880 the salt trade in Winsford was at its busiest and each black building shown on this map was a salt works. They crowded into the river valley on each side of the Weaver, which was the main route for delivering coal and exporting salt by barge. However branch lines and sidings ran on each side of the river to the backs of the works so that salt could be sent by rail to all parts of the country. Only during the twentieth century was New Road built for motor traffic to the area.

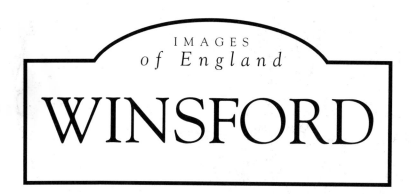

IMAGES
of England

WINSFORD

Compiled by
J. Brian Curzon

TEMPUS

First published 2001
Copyright © J. Brian Curzon, 2001

Tempus Publishing Limited
The Mill, Brimscombe Port,
Stroud, Gloucestershire, GL5 2QG

ISBN 0 7524 2274 X

Typesetting and origination by
Tempus Publishing Limited
Printed in Great Britain by
Midway Colour Print, Wiltshire

Cover illustration: A salt works, believed to be in Winsford.

Among the greatest changes to have taken place is the way we shop and spend our leisure time. At the time of this photograph the housewife would often shop daily, spending a few coins on small quantities of fresh ingredients for meals she prepared at home. Today cars, supermarkets and ready meals or takeaways have replaced shops like this. Making the most of a little was the main priority then; today shopping trips to buy with credit cards are a way of spending leisure time. The white stripes in the left window are sides of bacon stacked one on top of the other. Bacon was 6d or 8d a pound and was sliced while you watched! Between the glass and the display stand are pottery eggs which were used in shop window displays instead of fresh ones. They were placed so that hens laid next to them, where eggs could be easily collected. Biscuits in big tins are in the other window; they were weighed when wanted and put into a paper bag.

Contents

Acknowledgements

Many of the photographs that are included here are from my own collection. The Winsford Local History Society and the Winsford Library also placed their collections at my disposal. I am very pleased to record a long and happy working relationship with *The Chronicle*, whose photographers have skilfully copied old pictures for me.

Caveat

It is not intended to publish photographs 'for the first time' but to use them to tell the story of Winsford; and so some familiar views must be included to give you an idea of how things used to be between the 1880s and the 1980s – and to record 100 years of changes. It is impossible to say where the interior photos of salt works were taken and they are included to show the process even though some may not actually be Winsford works. The book is concerned with the town of Winsford in so far as it contained the older borough of Over, but it is not a history of Over.

Old Photographs

In Victorian times photographs were taken by professional photographers, usually in the form of studio portraits. However, sometimes they would attend at a special function or an unusual event such as a flood in the town to record it; these were then sold to people as souvenirs. The photographic paper used already had the words 'post card' printed on the back and so many 'post cards' may actually be the only photograph in existence showing that view and not one commercially produced. Some people would own a framed photograph of their home with their family outside which had been taken by a professional photographer. For a half penny – half the cost of a letter in an envelope – you could send a note and a local 'view' through the post. The Edwardian era was the great time for sending and collecting post cards; nowadays telephone calls and e-mail have replaced postcards for all but holiday messages.

The Brine Compensation Board commissioned a complete survey of the area of the town which was likely to be affected by subsidence, these were mainly taken in 1892 and have the details written on the negative which is included in the photograph. They were taken so that claims for damage after that date could be checked against the photograph.

Many pictures were taken in the nineteenth century where the photographer avoided including people altogether because they might move and this would spoil a photograph which needed quite some time to expose properly. For this reason people in old photographs often look stiff and serious. Group photographs have always been popular, but only in comparatively recent times were the people told to smile for the camera! With the growth of film cameras, the inter-war period saw the amateur being able to take their own informal snap-shots of people just relaxing.

Older photographs were taken on glass negatives at the actual size of the print, which often resulted in a very clear and detailed print. Modern photography is less clearly defined as the image is reduced onto the film and then enlarged to the size required. Because of this photographs taken to record the redevelopment in the 1970s are actually less suitable for reproduction than ones taken 100 years previously. Many recent photos are portraits rather than records of events or places and again are not really appropriate to reproduce. I have selected photographs to show aspects of a changing past for a generation to whom most of the subjects will be strange and obscure.

Introduction
The Way Things Used to Be

Cheshire is a county of contrast; along with historic market towns and pretty villages there are places which were developed in the industrial age of Queen Victoria. Like Crewe, Ellesmere Port, Runcorn or Widnes, Winsford was a product of the Victorian era and the story of Winsford can be told in old photographs.

Before the eighteenth century there was no town of Winsford, just a crossing point on the River Weaver. In 1721 Parliament allowed the Weaver to be made navigable, but it was not until the nineteenth century that the salt works in Winsford became profitable following the discovery of new brine supplies. Then Wharton developed as the area in which the salt workers lived and for a time the names Wharton and Winsford were used for the same place. Over, on the other hill, remained aloof until the two towns were joined, first by a Local Board of Health in 1874 and then in 1895 by the formation of the Urban District. However, rivalry between the two sides of the river persists. While it lacks old world charm, Winsford is a town which is well worth considering as an example of Victorian self assured development, showing how passing years changed its fortunes from prosperity to decline and back to prosperity again. These photographs also record changes in fashions and in the everyday life of a town once dominated by church and chapel or the pub.

As the salt works developed in what had previously been open countryside, there was need for new houses and these were built in Wharton. This town developed from a tiny hamlet at Wharton Green, in the parish of Davenham, to become a parish and township in its own right and a flourishing Victorian workers community. Winsford's lack of Christian worship and preference for the ale houses in the early days earned it a nickname of 'Dark Town' in the same context as 'Darkest Africa' but Victorian religious revivalism resulted in many new places of worship.

Occupation at the bottom of the hill, on the other side of the river, started in the early Victorian period, but it was not until the end of the nineteenth century and the Edwardian era that development all the way up the hill took place. The parallel streets created around the Over cotton mill, fustian factory and brick works, from the 1870s, represent an interesting Victorian industrial complex in an otherwise rural village. St George's Road, High Street and Swanlow Lane contain villas with large back gardens in which the middle classes of Victorian and Edwardian Winsford lived in houses looked after by servants. Those who lived on the hill at Over were respectable and religious, mainly middle class and considered themselves far superior to those manual workers in 'Dark Town' in the valley.

Winsford meant salt in the Victorian era. Its trade developed as that of Northwichs declined and it was a trade that depended on the river. The works lined the river for a mile and a half between Winsford Bridge and New Bridge. It was a hard and filthy trade. Every pan required its own chimney so Winsford has the dubious claim that there were more industrial chimneys in a mile than anywhere else on earth and the smoke helped create the impression of 'Dark Town' as it obscured the sun and the moon alike.

From a shanty town, a substantial Victorian new town grew up in the Wharton area; while the Over side of the river followed some years later. It was a rough and ready place, but slowly respectability and order emerged. The various branches of the Methodist church established places of worship with a strict Victorian code of abstinence from drink. The Methodists avoided the numerous beer houses that existed in the town. On the Over side, the further up the hill you lived the more likely you were to be considered 'posh' – and less likely to frequent an ale house – though there were over forty to pick from!

Prosperity for the workers followed slowly and in 1860 a Co-operative Retail Society brought their ideals of saving, self-help and investment to the town. After 1875 the Local Board provided fresh water from Oakmere which was pumped to the town. They replaced cesspits and bucket privies with flushing lavatories and sewers and provided street lights. Even so; the place was still visibly a 'Dark Town' because, to save the gas bill and discourage late night activities, the street lights were turned off after only a few hours! In 1901 it could still be described as 'The vilest hole' – a place where the smoke and smells were intolerable.

Many men went to war between 1914 and 1918 and women had to work in the jobs they had left behind. Salt was considered essential and during both world wars men who would not fight were conscripted to work in the local salt and 'munitions' factories which used salt as an ingredient in explosives. The Second World War brought evacuees, refugees, American servicemen and land girls all bringing changes to the way of life locally and some settled in the area.

From the 1930s attempts to bring new industry were made. A bacon factory for the Co-operative Retail Society was built on a site specially prepared for it by the council with its own railway side line for delivery. Old property was demolished as part of the Government's slum clearance policy. In Winsford this actually involved demolishing old half-timbered cottages which a decade or two later would have been listed as of special historic interest! They were replaced by council houses at first in places where old housing had been demolished, but later large housing estates were designed for a better, cleaner way of life.

In 1937 the Medical Officer of Health commented on the lack of births and an ageing population. He called for more children to be born. A decade later every woman of the right age was pushing a pram; as 'war babies' and the 'post-war bulge' created an urgent need for new houses, which were provided by the council. Winsford changed from 1961, when it became an overspill town – it was the only way to attract new investment. First people moved from Manchester and then from Liverpool – you can still hear those accents today in the town. At times in the '60s it was rather like *West Side Story* with Winsford, Liverpool and Manchester youths facing up to each other especially after a night drinking in a pub or at a dance.

The people who moved here in the '60s and '70s were young families intending to build new lives in their first real home in 'The Town in the Country' and others have followed. Some who moved from familiar neighbourhoods in the cities to live in the countryside found it was difficult adjusting to a different way of life and went back. Others stayed in the town determined to build a new and exciting way of life and the old was replaced by what was then considered to be modern. House building has not stopped in Winsford for half a century and today the town still attracts young families who find affordable homes within easy car journeys of shopping and leisure facilities. To those people these pictures will show a strange and unfamiliar place, but they may serve to explain why Winsford is the way it is.

These photographs record a town which vanished and was reborn. Here and there you can find buildings that can still be recognised. It is also a way of life that has vanished and is remembered here. Most photographs were taken between the 1880s and 1980s, but to those who attend school today they will seem a strange place – this was the 'Dark Town'.

One
The Weaver Navigation

In 1721, following the opening of docks at Liverpool in 1715 the Government allowed the Weaver to be deepened, widened and locks to be constructed so that barges could reach Winsford. From the early nineteenth century salt works lined the river so that coal could be unloaded and salt loaded onto barges which arrived black, and left white. A special sailing barge was used called a Weaver Flatt, which had a flat bottom for cargo. In the early days the crew would pull the barge along the towpath and then jump in to sail over the tidal Mersey estuary to Liverpool. During the 1870s railway branch lines opened into the salt works on either side of the river. As a reaction, the Weaver was improved and the number of locks was reduced while steam barges were introduced to provide adequate competition with the railways. It was at this time that the swinging New Bridge replaced the Butty Meadow Lock. Trade on the river declined after the big freeze in 1963 and after the closure of the railway branch lines a few years later the roads took over the town's transport needs. Any old Winsfordian will assure you that there are whales in the Weaver, but then point out in broad Cheshire they are 'yeld cart wales' (old cart wheels).

A busy scene on the Weaver over a century ago with the Town Bridge in the distance, the old town hall building. There is a sailing Weaver Flatt boat at Cross's Boat Yard on the right, these were the main transport for bringing Lancashire coal to the salt works and taking Winsford salt to Liverpool for export. The sail allowed them to cross the tidal river Mersey.

Because trade on the Weaver stopped on a Sunday during the religious revival of the Victorian era, a new church was built as a chapel of ease to St Chad's. Christ Church in Over was the waterman's church where they were always welcome. Unused at the start of redevelopment it was intended to be converted into an arts centre but vandals set the wood on fire making it unsafe.

Barges were loaded with salt from little piers outside the works from which the loose 'common salt' was tipped into the flat holds. There was continental involvement in the trade with Germans and Polish workers and factory owners. However, during the First World War the *Berlin* changed its name, and many German families left the Winsford district.

Salt works and barges, in the Meadow Bank area. Each one is a sailing flat with masts which were used for when crossing the tidal Mersey estuary; men usually pulled the barge to Runcorn. There was a busy trade and it was important to leave at the right time to catch the tide at Runcorn or a day could be lost waiting for the tide to return.

A busy time on the Weaver at a salt works, with salt being unloaded into a sailing flat, using the old spelling of *Burmah*. Much salt was exported to Asia and Africa and the name Lagos still survives in Winsford as a reminder of a vanished trade. In this picture it is bagged, fine salt which is being loaded, one class of this was called 'common Lagos'.

A sailing flat prepares to pass through the new bridge on its way into Winsford. The new bridge was built as a swing footbridge when the lock gates of the 'Butty Meadow' lock were removed, but the masonry of the lock remains. Beyond, the banks are without trees or grass while the Moulton Tunnel under the Crewe to Liverpool railway line can be seen on the left.

A stark picture of Verdin's Cut in the 1890s shows salt works and chimneys lining the river and by the works are masted-barges. The black and white medium only adds to the image of dark brooding industry, yet it was this trade which was responsible for the prosperity of Victorian Winsford and created the new town.

This view is similar to the previous one and of the same place but is worth including for the way in which it shows a barge with the curved covers removed from the hold on the left and with them in place on the right. The little boat was called a *cock boat* and was carried by all flat boats to act as a life boat in case of mishaps while crossing the tidal Mersey estuary.

The Flashes were created by pumping 'wild brine', so that the land sank at a distance from the salt works. In this way Winsford subsidence is different from that in central Northwich where disused mines collapsed. The Flash is still the central feature of Winsford and this 1960s scene shows it was popular for rowing, sailing and angling.

The Dock House, in the centre, was demolished in the 1960s when the present marina was created, in what had been Cross's Dock Yard, for building and repairing barges. Inside were pencil lines and dates written on one of the walls showing the height that flood waters had reached at various times.

This is a rather unusual view of the old town from the side of the Flash in the 1960s, it shows the Waterman's church reflected in the water. The gas tower was a fairly new structure then, but by the time of publication it may be just a memory as it is no longer used. In the distance is Weaver Street with the chapel in High Street beyond that.

One of the last remnants of water trade and the salt industry to be demolished was this timber structure which overhung the river near the Town Bridge in New Road. It was a covered store for salt with a section hanging over the river from where the salt could be tipped into the waiting barges. The salt store is pictured in the 1960s but lasted until 1997.

With a river in the middle, old Winsford was liable to flooding, especially as the ground at the centre had sunk as a result of salt subsidence. This postcard of the 1874 flood shows the old Market Place. The status of the men in the boat can be surmised; one of them is wearing a top hat and is believed to be the owner of the salt works on the left.

The same flood in Weaver Street, with the old Conservative Club on the right and a timber yard with stacks of planks on the right. It was due to this history of flooding in the valley that a decision to move the shops to the present site was taken during the 1960s.

Crowds always gathered to see something unusual and the photographer Thomas Dutton of Dingle Lane made these three photographs of the 1874 into postcards for people to buy. A plank walk has been created on the right where four brave men are standing, so that people could at least walk home from work if they lived on the other side.

The last flood to affect traffic in the town was in 1946, but by then motor traffic could get people across as the water level fell. Until it did, the only way to get from Over to Wharton was by going through Church Minshull or over Hartford Bridge. By that time Woolworth's, the old post office and other more solid shops had started a move away from the shanty town image.

The Conservative Club in Weaver Street (right) in the 1946 flood. The club was built on high foundations, to be above flood level, and several steps were needed to get in. Two people are standing on the top of the steps which are only just above flood level. The cloudy sky made photographing floods very difficult. The building in the distance is the Co-op.

Salt works still lined the river banks when the *Hondsrug* came to the Colin Stewart chemical works on 18 November 1949, to a reception by the chairman of the council. It was hoped that bringing the first ocean-going ship to Winsford would herald a new era for the post-war town, however river transport was at its end and lorries were to bring the new prosperity.

The tug *France Hayhurst* is slowly pulling the *Hondsrug* on the last stage of its journey into a Winsford which even in 1949 was still a busy salt producing town. The tug was named after the family from Bostock Hall who had at one time been merchants in Liverpool but settled at Bostock and took a leading hand in the Weaver Navigation management.

Two
The Salt Industry

There would have been no reason for a town to develop at Winsford at all had it not been that brine could be pumped close to the River Weaver, and from the early nineteenth century salt works developed to line the river from Winsford to the New Bridge. In them large 'pans' were used in which the liquid brine was heated to evaporate the water and form salt crystals. Different temperatures and periods of boiling produced an assortment of different crystal types. Salt mining is a different process in which solid salt is dug underground. Winsford mines were not very successful in the nineteenth century, but in 1928 an old mine was reopened following the collapse of the last mine in Northwich and is now the only mine in Britain from which rock salt, used to melt snow on the roads, is excavated. As all the salt works merged into a single company, and then production was moved to new works in Runcorn almost all trace of the industry has vanished. From the 1930s the local authorities have been keen to attract new industries to Winsford to replace the jobs which were lost as the salt works closed. The area which was once a forest of chimneys has been designated a part of the new Mersey Forest.

One of the most shocking images of old Winsford is this one, showing the salt works which lined the river in the 'Meadow Bank' area. As every pan required a square chimney to take away the smoke and fumes, and an open top to let the steam escape, the light of the sun was practically excluded. At its busiest there were almost 1,000 chimneys within a mile.

It is practically impossible to count the chimneys in this old view of Winsford's salt works, and yet this was published as a postcard! Many people came to see the works and discover how salt was made. This view shows the barges on the river and salt wagons on the railway sidings ready to transport the finished salt to all parts of the Empire.

Meadow, Uploont & Stubbs' Salt Works, Winsford from the Air.

This aerial view of the Weaver north of the bridge shows the original course of the Weaver and how Verdin's cut made a straighter route for bigger boats, creating The Island at the centre. On the left the Cheshire lines railway curves to avoid passing through Vale Royal Park. This is probably sometime in the 1920s as works in the foreground have been demolished.

Before 1870 salt works were places which caused concern for morality. This painting by Philip Horman Miller sends subtle messages of the dangers – physical and moral. Men working half naked by the fires and sleeping where there was danger from hot ashes or scalding brine and a woman close by breast feeding a baby during a break from work is watched by the men.

The size of salt pans can be judged by this picture. The rakes worked best with handles 15ft long so most pans were 30ft wide for easy use. Men always worked stripped to the waist because of the heat and while some Victorians found this obscene, others visited the salt works keen to see well-built naked torsos in an age where bodies were usually covered.

From the 1870s women were not allowed to work by the salt pans by law, instead many of them became packers. Salt was one of the first products to come in cardboard boxes as it was difficult to store loose salt in a shop. This photograph is obviously 'staged' as everyone has crammed in to be included. The women in the foreground are sewing up bags of salt with string.

More women sew bags of salt. As they were paid for the number of bags they sewed they would take the string home with them and cut it into lengths, then tie the knot on one end as they walked to work, keeping the pieces tucked in a belt. Salt in bags like this was sent to Africa and African labels are on some bags while others are reused sugar bags!

The start of the process of salt making was the stoking of huge hearths under the pans. They used coal from St Helens which was generally of a poor quality and gave off foul sulphurous smoke therefore rendering it unsuitable for domestic use. Often men from the same family would share the work taking it in turns to stoke or to catch a few hours sleep on the floor in the ashes.

The exterior of a salt works was unmistakable. Above each pan was a roof with an open top to let the steam escape. Each one had its own chimney, and because the salt was corrosive to brick, only the parts under the pan were made of brick the rest were made of wooden planks. The steam kept the wood damp and helped to reduce the fire risk.

The salt pan is shown in the foreground, where 'rafts' of salt crystals can be clearly seen floating on the brine. As the heat removed water in the form of steam, crystals of salt form and join together until the mass is so heavy that it sinks. The man beyond is using a long handled rake to bring the crystals to the side to be shovelled out and dried.

This postcard was posted on 9 July 1904 and shows two pans being worked side by side. Salt making required skill and a steady hand, as well as muscle. This worker is tipping the salt from the wooden tubs; the warm crystals bonded together so the whole became a solid block which was taken to the hot house for thorough baking. Often salt was sold as a block or cut into the size of a loaf for grinding in the kitchen, although by 1900 ready-ground salt in packets was available.

24

Loading the two-wheeled barrows, which were used to take common salt to the waiting barges or railway wagons. It needed great skill to tip the barrows and not to be thrown into the vessel below, a number of deaths and casualties due to this are recorded. The men wear clogs, but the trousers are cut short to avoid getting wet and salty which would dissolve the cloth.

Another view of the same men clearly showing the wooden soled clogs. The wooden bars above the pans were intended to prevent accidents to workers who might loose their footing and fall into the boiling brine. Such accidents inevitably proved fatal. The basic working conditions with whitewashed walls and rough wood floors are a stark contrast to modern factories.

A procession of two-wheeled barrows takes the common salt to a waiting barge. The men almost invariably worked without shirts because of the heat so women were kept away from them, however, children were given a half hour extra at lunch time to take their father's meals and a supply of ale or a soft drink (depending on their religion) to them in the works.

A related industry was the building and repairing of boats for use on the river. There were six boat yards which eventually merged into the Salt Union. Here, the *Monarch* is being launched into the Weaver. Local vessels were always launched sideways as they were longer than the river was wide.

This picture was among a group of glass negatives of scenes in Winsford that were given to the author and passed on to the Salt Museum. It was difficult to work out exactly what was depicted but it actually shows the effect of salt subsidence on an important industrial feature needed to store and clean the brine allowing grains of sand to sink to the bottom.

The Salt Museum kindly provided this picture of what the cleaning process would have looked like when functioning. It is part of a brine cistern used to allow the brine to stand so that sand and other impurities settle out of the liquid. The fountain like appearance is akin to something from a Victorian holiday postcard from the sea side.

The creation of the Salt Union ended competition between factory owners to attract workers, as almost all people working in the salt works or on the river worked for the same company which paid the same wages and expected the same hours. In 1892 this caused so much unrest that 100 policemen and 100 soldiers were required to restore order during a strike.

Although Winsford had its own fire engine known as Albert (after the Prince Consort, as was the infirmary), which is now exhibited in the Yorkshire Carriage Museum, the Salt Union also maintained its own engine as fires in the works were not uncommon and could spread quickly through dry wooden buildings. This horse-drawn engine has a steam powered pump.

An early picture of the Salt Mine at Meadow Bank. This started up in the 1840s but proved unsuccessful and closed down. In 1928 it was reopened as rock salt was found to be ideal for melting snow on the road. Here men are using shovels and wheelbarrows to carry the salt from the face to the railway line which took it to the lift.

A special cutting machine in the 1930s, which, the caption states, was similar to those used in coal mines. As rock salt is harder than coal the cutters would wear out more quickly than in a coal mine despite being made of specially hardened metal. Note how the workmen wear caps even though they are underground and away from rain and sun.

It looks like a great mountain range and, until recently, visiting Meadow Bank incurred a strange feeling of walking in outer space – so much so that it was used as such for TV science fiction series! More modern methods of loading now allow the salt to be put straight in to waiting lorries and the vast stock piles of days gone by are no more.

Herman Falk dug the first salt mine and operated it in the 1840s. He is still remembered for bringing foreign labour to Winsford to break strikes and for being the driving force in creating the Salt Union. However hated his name was locally, it nevertheless stood for quality and was used by the Salt Union for marketing until it was absorbed by ICI – as this 1920s delivery van shows.

Another 1920s aerial view, which must have been taken on Sunday when all the fires were turned out under the pans. They were cleaned when cool on Monday and housewives took the advantage of a smokeless day to try to get their washing dry. The effect of the mergers to form the Salt Union can be judged by comparing this view to the salt works on the map (see p. 2).

The brine was pumped into reservoirs to allow impurities to settle. The brine pipe, left, is shown emptying into a reservoir by the salt mine, which can be seen in the distance. By the time the last salt was made in Winsford it was actually pumped to the town from controlled borings at Holford so that the risk of subsidence and damage to the mine was avoided.

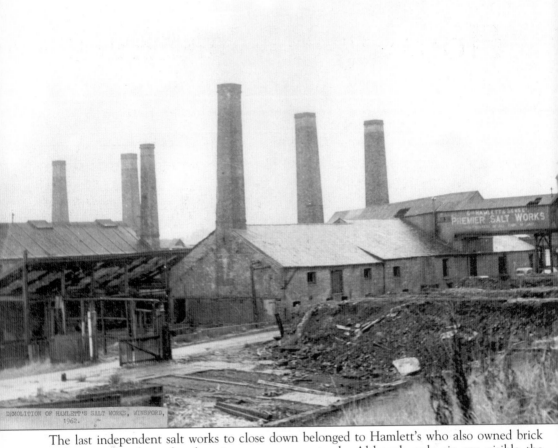

DEMOLITION OF HAMLETT'S SALT WORKS, WINSFORD, 1962.

The last independent salt works to close down belonged to Hamlett's who also owned brick making works where the shopping centre now stands. Although only six are visible the chimneys were known as the Seven Sisters of Winsford until they were demolished. The name Lagos Close is a reminder of the trade the firm had with West Africa.

Three
Housing the Workers

Around 1,000 people were engaged in salt making in Winsford by 1851 and they needed somewhere to live; as did all those working in other trades. A new town was developed in the Wharton area, during the nineteenth century. Unlike Crewe to the south, which was developed by the railway company as a planned town at the same time, Wharton was a series of developments made by small investors building houses to let or to sell. The houses were built slightly to the south of the salt works to avoid the winds which usually carried the smoke to the east. Because of the unsteady nature of the ground, which could be undermined by salt subsidence, the houses tended to be built in pairs rather than in long rows. In Over four parallel streets were built in the 1870s. Over 2,000 sub-standard homes were demolished in a few years of 'slum clearance' in the '30s. Much of the older housing is villa-style from the late Victorian and Edwardian period of prosperity in the town, while the majority dates from the second half of the twentieth century. In the 1960s it was used as an overspill town and large estates were built at that time. It is ironic that the little nineteenth-century workers' cottages which were meant to be replaced by council houses became those which 'first time buyers' purchased to move out of the council estates and get on the property ladder – with council grants to improve them.

Slum clearance was responsible for robbing the district of a heritage of half timbered houses. Faced with Government regulations on the conditions allowed for human habitation the council had no option but to demolish property like this block in Delamere Street which were built when well water and cesspits were acceptable and people cooked on the open fire.

This seventeenth-century thatched cottage was demolished in the 1973 to be replaced with a row of ordinary looking shops. Next to it can be seen Over Cross and the former Market Hall which became a charity school in the 1840s and later the Church of England School. Some of the beams were used to make partitions in Knight's Grange when it was converted to a pub.

The timber-framed construction was obvious when the demolition started but by then it was too late to preserve the house as an attractive feature – as it was not listed there had been no objection to demolishing it. Hazelnut shells were found in the thatch which showed evidence of dormice. Finding dormice anywhere is highly unlikely in today's Winsford!

The only clue that this house in Delamere Street once had a thatched roof is the lighter coloured brickwork on the wall of the next building, which was protected from smoke by the thatch. The projecting chimney shows that another room was demolished from the left and that it was once a three-roomed thatched cottage – the half timber is preserved inside.

The corrugated iron roof of this old cottage was put over a thatch around a century ago. During the seventeenth century it was a three-roomed half-timbered farmstead but during the early nineteenth century it was split to form three separate tiny houses and later one of them served as a general shop. It has been replaced by a similar shaped construction but with modern services.

One of the few timber-framed houses to survive is the Dawk House on Swanlow Lane. This former farm of 1711 was split into three dwellings during the housing shortage of the nineteenth century but later restored to create a single home in the more prosperous area of the town. The wing to the left originally contained a dairy at ground floor level at the back.

These men were restoring Dawk House in the 1930s and show how even on a building site men would wear a hat and jacket. Informal clothing only became common during the 1960s and it was not until the heat waves of the '70s that people would think of working without a shirt, except in the exceptional heat of the salt works, or wearing shorts for anything but sport.

A car sales agency now occupies this site in Delamere Street. The Over mews was the equivalent of a car hire or a taxi firm at the time, where horses and carriages could be hired from behind the half-timbered cottage – which was demolished in the 1950s. The Over Brewery used natural spring water to make beer, which was consumed by thirsty salt workers.

Delamere Street is built above a thick layer of sand trapped in clay which acted as the reservoir for old Over. The building on the left was used as a lemonade factory, using well water. Inferior brickwork, right of the central door, shows this was once three small cottages. It was upgraded when Newton, the chemist, opened a shop in one and lived in the others.

Another vanished necessity of the time when horses provided the power was the smithy. This one was in Delamere Street where Saxon Crossway is now. It was part of the Delamere Estate until 1911, when it was sold to C.W.W. Richardson for £620. The two-wheeled cart is a 'floater', with a low floor for loading beer barrels or churns of milk.

The Vale Royal Sale Catalogue of 1911 informs us that this building contained two dwellings, one of them functioning as a small shop as well. Today it is restored and its half-timber construction has been revealed by removing the cement rendering. It stands opposite the Gate Inn a name which is derived from the old English 'yate', meaning high road, not a toll gate.

Herman Falk rented land near Newbridge in the 1840s where he dug the salt mine and operated salt works. Notorious for bringing in foreign labour to break strikes he had to build houses for them to live in. The famous Bass Houses were built using the slag from the furnaces. Notice the cage by the door for a wild bird, to be used as a lure in a trap. A captive male bird was put in a cage to attract the females, which would be captured with nets or on bird lime. In a pie they made a popular meal.

This old couple outside one of the Bass Houses look blissful, but the poor conditions and rooms where people of all ages and both sexes would sleep together on the floor in the only clothes they had meant that there were many health risks. Lack of sanitation helped to cause the last outbreak of cholera in this area in 1866. The houses were demolished as slums after the Second World War though, in their defence, they were said to be warm and cosy.

More inhabitants of the Bass Houses around the turn of the nineteenth century. They do not seem to show any signs of the appalling conditions recorded here during the cholera crisis when the houses were rented to immigrant workers. Bricks were used to make frames around the doors and windows, but the main walls are of bass covered with a cement rendering.

With no planning and no need to conform to plans because there were no sewers, water, gas nor electricity supplies to consider, houses could be built in any available position. The builder used a standard house plan to build singly, in pairs or in straight rows. As a result this picture gives the illusion that one of the cottages has come loose and slipped down the hill.

The growing town needed new houses and while some were built by landlords to rent and others were provided by the town's building society some were very much a 'do it yourself' affair. This building still stands in Weaver Street. It cost less to build three walls than four and so it was added onto the end of the existing row – the builder still gave it an 1862 date stone!

It was said that the further up High Street you lived, the better off you were. This was one of the lowest houses down the hill at No. 77! Photographs like this, of someone standing outside their house or on the door step, were very common in Victorian times as grown-up children would buy them when they married to remind them of their childhood home and their parents.

41

Some idea of housing conditions can be gained from this postcard just before the First World War. It shows the author's grandparents' entire family outside their terraced house on the right. Seeing a photographer at work was unusual and all the family poured out onto the pavement to watch when High Street was photographed.

A record of the effects of salt subsidence in the town centre. The pair on the left were built of brick before the nature of subsidence was understood and the ground (with them on it) has sunk, but the road outside has been raised to the original level. The timber-framed building next to it could be 'lifted' by putting jacks under it and building new foundations.

Winsford's worst problem was subsiding land as brine was pumped from under the soil. A regular feature in the old town were metal plaques like the one shown in the centre of this picture which held rods that went through the building and prevented walls from falling outwards as the land under the foundations gave way.

A different sort of plaque is shown on this house. Policing was still a locally organized affair and the plaque indicated that a policeman lived there who could be called upon in an emergency. The more elaborate house to the right is of timber-framed construction, designed to be raised on jacks in case the land underneath subsided.

Many houses in Wharton were built in pairs so that they could move without affecting the whole row. Notice how the houses on either side of the taller pair have tipped towards it. Fences were not always permanent and could be ripped out if coal was short and a fire was needed! Most of these houses have outside privies in the sloping gardens.

Many older people remember Winsford as a long street of more or less continuous rows of houses from the station to Over Square. The most striking thing about this picture of Station Road compared to the same place today is the lack of parked cars which now usually line the road. Old Winsford was not designed for motor traffic and new roads were essential to redevelopment.

At the other end of town Victoria Terrace was built on rising land near Over Square facing High Street, so a retaining wall was needed in front. To prevent children running about and playing on the long paved areas in front a series of walls were built so that each section was approached from its own set of steps ensuring quiet and privacy.

The building of this huge cotton mill in 1870 was intended to bring alternative work to the salt trade but fire destroyed it in 1874. The nearby houses from Geneva Road (once Factory Street) to Dean Street were intended for the workers but eventually housed brick makers and salt workers in an industrial hamlet complete with shops, chapels and pubs.

The fire gutted the spinning mill, but the single-story weaving shed remained for many years as a fustian cutting room. The men leaning on the fence in this picture are not mill workers – part of the roof has been demolished and they are obviously taking down the mill to replace it with a factory which made model trains at the time it was destroyed, also by fire, in the 1990s.

When the factory chimney was demolished several professional photographers recorded the fall and their pictures were soon on sale as souvenirs. The so called 'chimney houses', a group of six dwellings in Upper Haigh Street, were built in 1914 using the bricks. There can have been little ill feeling towards the mill owner, as his name was used for them.

To try to attract new industry to the town the Co-operative Retail Society made contact with the Wholesale Society who undertook to build a bacon factory on a site that the council would prepare for it, by the railway line, with its own sidings to bring live pigs to it. This architect's drawing shows it as a factory in a garden setting and is from the Coronation souvenir of 1937.

In 1945, almost as soon as the war ended, work was started on new housing developments. To provide emergency housing for the de-mobbed soldiers and their families, concrete prefabricated bungalows were built where they could live while the new houses were constructed. Kingsway, shown here, was on one side of the river and Queensway on the other.

Men at work on the new council houses in Wharton. Different housing styles were used to avoid monotony, they were set in irregular groups with grass spaces to create 'village greens' as play areas. Every house had a large garden as people were encouraged to continue growing vegetables as they had done in the war. Wharton church tower is in the background.

This picture was published in 1945 with the caption 'what not to do with a new council house'. The new tenant had built an improvised shed and was keeping chickens in Kingsway. Brick coal houses and sheds were provided in order to prevent this on the Dene. Only a few years previously people had been encouraged to keep chickens because of wartime food shortages.

Different plans of houses and the use of painted and plain brickwork gave variety to the Dene estate, while the open square in Sycamore Avenue can be seen to the right. Originally old trees were left to help create a countryside feel and every street was named after the trees that were growing in it. This is a view from Cherry Crescent which still has its cherry blossom in spring.

Older property, built early in the twentieth century and set in garden plots along Delamere Street in the foreground, with the Grange Estate which was the first one to be built for overspill during the 1960s. It was affectionately called 'The Ponderosa' after the ranch in a TV series. This aerial photograph in 1974 shows how closely the estate houses were built.

When these houses were built many people called the area a toy town, because they looked like a row of perfect dolls' houses set behind their access road parallel to Swanlow Lane. They were a complete contrast to the small terraces or large villas of pre-war Winsford. New houses in the overspill years of the '60s sold for around £2,000 each.

Crook Lane estate was one of the first to use prefabricated house parts to create identical council housing units again. Brick was used for separating walls and to reduce noise from the neighbours, but the front and back of each house were factory made and assembled quickly on site. They had no chimneys, as they were centrally heated, and looked strange because of this.

There was a special reason to take this photograph of new houses in Nixon Drive. When they were built in 1970 the Over hoard of silver coins in a black mug was found when back-filling a drain trench. The coins dated from around 1643 and are believed to have been hidden during the Civil War. Declared 'Treasure Trove', the mug and coins are now in the Grosvenor Museum in Chester.

Contrasting developments are shown clearly in this 1974 aerial view with private housing, set in their own gardens, in the centre and the flat roofs and white painted walls of the so-called 'White Cliffs of Over'. These were council-owned estates for the overspill population from Liverpool and were built using new and untried building methods.

The Victorian census returns record 'licensed hawkers' living in horse-drawn caravans with their children on the banks of the Flashes. Today there are luxury caravan developments at various places around the town. In the inter-war period the caravan sites were often nothing more than shanty towns which were removed under slum clearance regulations.

Winsford still has some mysteries. For instance why this group of houses in Station Road has always been known as 'Skin Pudding Row'. One possible reason is a tale relating that each Sunday, one of the inhabitants made a huge rice pudding for all to share. They have large front gardens from an age when growing vegetables in the front garden was normal.

A recent aerial view of the Wharton area showing School Road and Princess Street. The houses are interesting as even in the mid-nineteenth century they were built with quite large rear gardens for growing vegetables and in pairs as a precaution against fire and salt subsidence. It is actually an important early planned community. Old Wharton School can be seen in the top right corner.

Finding an ideal home in Winsford created unexpected solutions. This postcard of 1906 records a floating home on the Flashes, complete with curtains and a life belt. It was surrounded by a fence to prevent occupants accidentally stepping off the floating island, but one wonders how they coped with necessities such as a need for drains!

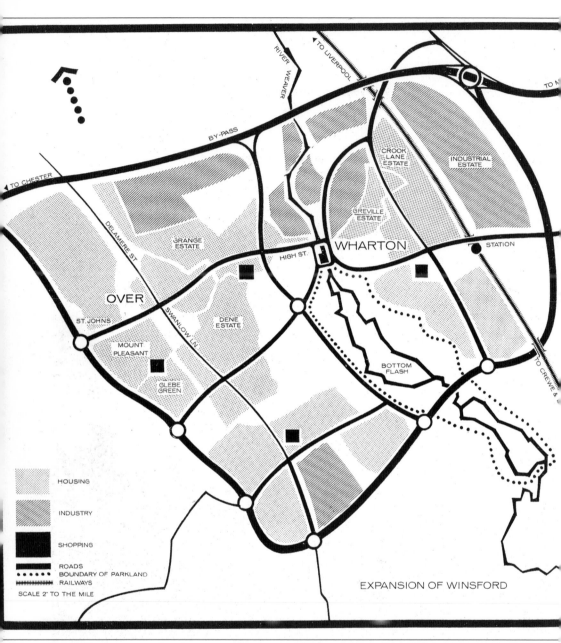

In 1962 extensive development plans were drawn up to allow Winsford to expand to accommodate more than 70,000 people. The areas to be developed were zoned so that industry and housing were kept apart, while the centre of the town, which had been affected by subsidence and flooded, was abandoned to be made into parkland. A ring road was planned but never completed.

Four

Shopping

Today many people travel out of town to shop in big centres where there is plenty of choice. For previous generations there was no option but to buy locally and many small shops existed just a short walk from the customer's homes; these were often converted rooms in terraced houses. Most women shopped every day for the needs of that day, paying with cash. Workers were all paid in cash and few had bank accounts. There was nowhere to store food for long in the days before refrigerators. In 1860 a shopping revolution came to Winsford when the Co-operative Retail Society was formed which shared profits amongst its customer members as 'divi'. Eventually it developed a variety of specialist shops in the High Street and branches existed in many parts of the district which offered a greater selection than the local shops but within easy carrying distance – which was important when no one owned a car. Supermarkets arrived at the Co-op shops in 1960 and in the mid-1960s a new shopping centre was built. This brought new shops and supermarket chains to the town and for the first time the idea of driving to the shops was normal. During the 1990s out of town shopping has been provided on a site in Wharton for large stores with their own car parks, cafés and even banking, where people will buy food to stock freezers for months at a time.

There has been trading in Over for 700 years, ever since the Abbot of Vale Royal granted a charter to hold a weekly market and two fairs a year. The fairs were for selling livestock and this old postcard records one in Edwardian days where stalls were set up outside the Black Bear pub and crowds could stand in Delamere Street without traffic worrying them.

Winsford's Market Hall backed onto the river in Market Place and in this Victorian photograph the furniture shop with wooden chairs and iron bedsteads on the right is of interest. When the market closed down it was transformed first as The Strand Ballroom and later Mr Smith's Club which, by the 1960s, provided dancing and other entertainment including striptease nights.

The town hall was run by the same company as the market who rented the ground floor as shops, which look rather gloomy in an age before electric lights. The rents ensured a regular weekly income to pay for the upkeep of the assembly room above. The Co-op's riverside warehouse is seen over the river down the alleyway at the side.

One of the most interesting groups of buildings was Breeze's Forge on the High Street which was originally the Primitive Methodist Sunday School. It was later used as the Church of England infants' school, before the school moved to Gladstone Street, after which it was used as a forge. The shops were added in the early twentieth century and you can see the way they were added.

Winsford had an early Co-operative Society, which was formed in 1860; this was the first shop which stood near the bridge. When it was being built a man stopped to ask who it was being built for and when told it was for profit sharing he remarked 'Who'd have thought it'. This was used as the motto of the society and included on the plaque above the door.

The original Co-operative Shop is on the right of this picture, showing how the road had to be raised to counter subsidence. Rubbish was not normally left in the middle of the road and is probably from repair work in one of the shops awaiting collection. To the left are the boot and shoe department and the household goods department in separate shops.

As a comparison, and to show the effect of subsidence in the old town centre, this picture of the same shops was taken some years earlier and shows that at that time you went up steps to get to them. By the time the previous picture was taken the pavement was 18 inches below the road level. Notice the rolls of lino for floor covering by the door.

In 1910 the Co-op marked its Golden Jubilee and a special plate was issued with holes in the back for string to hang it on the wall. The picture shows the central store and office at the corner of Weaver Street with the butcher's next to it on the right. Upstairs were the offices where every member's transactions were recorded and their 'dividend' was calculated.

This photograph is from the 1970s, before the demolition of the south side of High Street, and shows the furnishing department and the ladies department of the Co-op boarded up and ready for the demolition workers, as are the other shops. On the left is the single story 'Gas Works Show Rooms' where the latest devices in household appliances were shown.

The Co-operative main building was redesigned in 1960 to create a new furnishing and shoe department on either side of a covered entrance which served as a bus shelter. The grocery department became the town's first self-service shop and the windows are full of posters advertising special offers. Heavy traffic and two bus stops made this a dangerous road.

When the town launched its overspill drive a competition was held to find Winsford's Happy Mother. The winner was used to advertise the advantages of living in the developing town to possible newcomers from Merseyside. Here she and her daughter are selecting which sort of tea to drink in the Co-op's self-service shop – notice it came in quarter pound packets in the 1960s!

Vandalism is not a new phenomenon. In Victorian times many shops put wooden shutters over their windows at night to protect the glass from drunks or thieves who might break it. The boards can clearly be seen stored to the left of this shop window on Hill Street, which was considered one of the more superior streets in Victorian Winsford.

Most of the old shops were quite literally corner shops; this building on the corner of New Road and High Street went through various owners and uses. Notice how the owner has merely added his name to the top of the sign of the previous owner and added the word 'late'. It was a grocer and off-licence around 1900 which sold Australian wines and Irish whisky.

The sign on Bitwistle's, at the end of Woodford Lane, says it sold fireplaces. The shop still does – but not much else remains the same. Most of the contents seem to have been taken out for display on the pavement and fences in this posed photograph of around 1900. A reminder of the time is the range of tin baths hanging above the windows and the metal buckets above.

It is interesting to compare the ideas of a 'complete house furnishing shop' with today's do it yourself stores. An iron mangle to force water out of washing is on the left, there are tin baths of different sizes and small patterned rugs on display. The last line of the advertisement shows that things could be 'put on side' to be paid for in instalments and taken home when paid for.

There is an interesting contrast in this view of the north of High Street. Chester's also has ironmongery on display on the pavement, which was normal in pre-war days. Among the display are scythe handles, garden forks and lawn rakes and a more rural range of goods even though it was nearer to the salt works. Next to it the shop is empty and the windows are shuttered.

There seemed to be references to Imperial Rome in the name of this shop as SPQR Stores – but in fact the initials stood for 'small profits, quick returns' and were intended to indicate low prices inside. There was never a graveyard in High Street; the stones on the right are the stock in trade of a monumental mason, ready made gravestones waiting for inscriptions.

In today's age of the internet the notice above Harry Oaks' window advertising 'wireless supplies' seems quaint and requires some explanation. The wireless was an old name for a radio as it did not need connecting to a wire like a phone. The window is full of bikes and enamelled signs advertise motor oil. The shop was next to the Waterman's church on High Street.

Williams' was a long established printers on the lower part of the High Street, he was also a newsagent as the bill boards show. The advertisement in the window is for 'stove ornaments' which were the sort of pottery figures and vases made in vast quantities in Staffordshire, essential on every Victorian mantlepiece! This shy little boy is unusual for not wanting his photograph taken.

This store was one of many built entirely of timber in the town centre, which resembled the wild west in this respect. On the top are ventilators which allowed stale air to escape but did not cause draughts which would help to spread a fire in a wooden building. Fashion tastes are indicated by the advertisement for mantles, that is the draped lace head coverings of widows.

The Victorian working class shopper would buy a few ounces or pounds of ingredients each day and wanted shops close by from which to carry them home. Many were like this one – little more than a converted front room of a house with a larger window to display items. On sunny days the roller blinds were pulled down to protect the items inside from the light and heat.

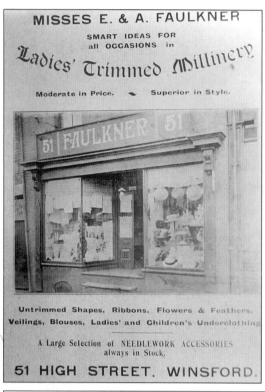

MISSES E. & A. FAULKNER

SMART IDEAS FOR
all OCCASIONS in

Ladies' Trimmed Millinery

Moderate in Price. ~ Superior in Style.

Untrimmed Shapes, Ribbons, Flowers & Feathers.
Veilings, Blouses, Ladies' and Children's Underclothing

A Large Selection of NEEDLEWORK ACCESSORIES
always in Stock,

51 HIGH STREET. WINSFORD.

Running a shop was an acceptable way for unmarried middle class women to earn a living and should they marry they would at once give up earning to look after the house and family. Millinery was one of the most respectable of things to sell as your hat was a sign of status and the wealthiest women had the biggest hats, as can be seen in other photographs.

This advertisement from a town guide of the 1950s has a tale to tell. The owner wanted to show that his shop offered service and civility and so joined the two words. He did not check with a dictionary for the word 'servility' actually refers to serfdom and slavery – it in fact implied a slave market! Note what the idea of groceries was around fifty years ago!

SERVICE AND SATISFACTION

(ORDERS DELIVERED)

SERVILITY STORES

HIGH CLASS GROCERIES and PROVISIONS

243 WEAVER STREET, WINSFORD

Cliff Dickenson's is known today as a motor repair and sales business, but it started in a bike shop in Station Road in an age when everyone cycled everywhere. The enamelled metal signs and white window letters were popular forms of advertising. The 'safety bicycle' on the left replaced 'penny farthings' in the 1890s – the name implied you were less likely to fall off one.

When this photograph was shown to a group of children to illustrate the shocking state of the roads and the old pathway up the side of Wharton Hill, the thing they found most repulsive was the dead sheep hanging outside the butcher's shop. In an age of refrigeration and pre-packed food they had never seen meat displayed in this way, which was once considered normal.

The first omnibus ran in 1914, and in the years after the First World War frequent services developed with regular links for the town with Northwich (where this bus was based) Crewe, Chester, Manchester and Hanley so that out of town shopping and visits to places of entertainment were possible. As cars became more usual these services gradually diminished.

With the building of the new shopping centre in the '60s a large Co-operative department store opened at the centre from which it was possible to buy just about anything. However, the Co-op felt the competition when new supermarket chains opened and the Winsford Society was taken over by one based in Birkenhead, who eventually ended over 100 years of trading.

Shops with dwellings upstairs were as much of a feature of the new shopping area, built in the mid-1960s, as they had been in the old. At its heart was a large fountain, which proved very unpopular as the wind blew the spray onto shoppers.

The fountain was eventually permanently switched off after numerous complaints and there was talk of making it into a flower bed instead. The girls would not sit so close in the days when it was working but the name Fountain Square remains. The backs of houses in the old part of High Street can be seen.

Old Winsford had a second shopping centre at Over Square, or Four Lane Ends, where you could buy most things. It is shown here at the end of the 1960s with a rock garden where Dr Okell's surgery and house once stood. Today the rockery is replaced by 'Over Square Roundabout'; the joke is, of course, that it is neither round nor square.

The real tuck shop for the secondary schools in Winsford was 'Jasper Parry's' which was almost opposite the schools. There you could buy single cigarettes or a glass of pop to be consumed inside, or snacks to take to the school yard. It has been impossible to find a photograph of it, but this shop on Grange Lane will serve as a reminder, with its jars of sweets and chewing gum machines outside.

The shopping centre is being built in the background of this 1960s view showing Chapel Street after the houses had been cleared. There was a small Primitive Methodist chapel but when that was vacated it was rented by the Catholic Church. However, the congregation could not afford the rent and Mass was held in the Guildhall by priests from Middlewich.

There is always change in the town, this picture shows the open entrance from Dene Drive. The war memorials were moved from High Street to be in a safer position in the middle of the shops where there was shelter on wet Remembrance Days. By the 1990s the risk of vandalism on the centre had grown so that doors were erected and locked at night.

This once busy section of High Street, which had churches, shops, banks and cafés, is now a road to nowhere without a single building left standing. Planners of the redevelopment seemed determined to erase as much of old Winsford as they could.

This dramatic picture records the demolition of the lower part of High Street and the old blue-brick retaining wall of Wharton Hill. The wall on the right was made from stone sleepers used in George Stephenson's original railway line through the district in 1837. Only a few buildings such as the Red Lion, Pimlotts former shop and the old chapel remain standing in 2001.

Five

Churches and Chapels

Churches and chapels played a much more important role in life in the past. Up to the middle of the twentieth century people went to them as much for the warmth and companionship as faith, and they provided a wide range of social activities. Sunday schools and church halls allowed people to meet others away from the tiny overcrowded houses in which they lived. On Sundays, the day of rest, there was little else to do other than attend a church service. The salt works developed away from any church provision and the first salt workers spent the whole week in the factory, few attending at any place of worship. As the town developed new facilities were provided, aiming to bring the light of religion into 'Dark Town'. Wharton acquired a new church to replace the former chapel which was demolished to make way for the railway in 1837, and it became a new parish. A second new parish was created at St John's in Over as people were attending local nonconformist chapels rather than travelling to St Chad's. In Victorian times yearly rents were charged for the use of pews there, so working people preferred the chapels where the seating was free. The Methodists opened chapels in the new industrial areas as well as the countryside so that worshippers did not have to walk far in bad weather and many signed the pledge not to touch alcohol. The Salvation Army flourished in late Victorian Winsford. There were few Catholics until the arrival of workers from Liverpool and Manchester, with Irish origins, in the 1960s. Mass was held in a former stables in Ways Green. Older residents who had attended strictly teetotal chapels were shocked when attending a funeral at the new St Joseph's Catholic church to find it had its own bar in the adjoining club!

This aerial view of St Chad's shows how the oldest church in Winsford is also its remotest. It was already in existence when the borough was founded around 1300 and people wanted to be buried near their ancestors. New houses could be built, but the traditional burial ground was not moved. Notice the original circular shape of the churchyard.

It is clear to see from the change in the quality of the stone how St Chad's was extended in 1926 to make a memorial to the Winsford men who died in the First World War. The older sixteenth-century wall was rebuilt using the original stone from the church and is now much wider and longer than the original church.

The sixteenth-century tower of St Chad's shows the light coloured square face of a former clock. Inside a plaque recalls how the vicar, Edward Moore, was killed when the works fell on him. In the eighteenth century a boy was sent to pinch a piece from the old yew at midnight for a dare and witnessed grave robbing here; he was sent to give evidence at Chester Assizes.

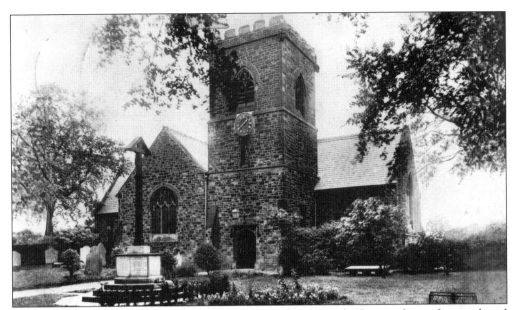

Wharton was created as a new parish. The present church was built to replace a former chapel which served Wharton and Bostock and was demolished to make way for the railway line in 1837. It is an unusual structure which forms a perfect cross with a tower in one corner on the north side but not the west end. From a postcard dated 5 October 1937.

Built as a memorial to the late Lady Delamere between 1860 and 1863, St John's contains her monogram in several places. It was built to cater for a growing population who were attending Methodist services closer to home rather than having to travel on the dirty footpath over the Town Fields to St Chad's. The chimney on the left was used for central heating to keep the congregation warm!

The original Waterman's church was built out of the profits from trade on the River Weaver, for workmen to worship no matter where they were on the river. There are matching churches at Runcorn and Northwich. In 1881 dangerous cracks were seen and this contemporary engraving shows crowds gathered as if they were expecting it to fall after it was declared unsafe.

A contemporary engraving of the interior shows the metal tie bars used to support the walls, but plaster has fallen from the walls to expose the brickwork and it was considered too dangerous to be used. It was replaced by a timber-framed structure but that too was considered beyond repair in the 1970s although there had been hopes to use it as an arts centre.

John Douglas designed the impressive 'stripy' congregational church on Swanlow Lane. This postcard is dated 1905 and shows the old white cottage which was demolished around forty years ago and the former manse beyond. On the left is the garden wall of Dr Okell's house where he held his surgery. It was cleared and eventually replaced by 'Over Square Roundabout'.

Methodist meetings were at first held in people's homes and this photograph from the Bethesda anniversary booklet has a caption to say that one of the cottages, by Wharton Bridge, was the first home of the Primitive Methodist Movement in Winsford. Meetings were held in the cottage of John Hickson before 1835 when plans for a real chapel were made.

The Primitive Methodist church on Station Road opened in 1865, but by the time of this picture, in 1892, it had become unsafe due to salt-mine subsidence and awaited rebuilding. The present timber-framed Bethesda chapel opened in 1894.

One of the biggest preaching houses and Sunday school complexes belonged to the United Methodist Free Church in the High Street which was often used as the town's concert hall for productions of the *Messiah* and other choral works as it was the largest and most central chapel. An observer writing in 1937 commented, 'you get good singing in Winsford'.

This male voice choir is outside the entrance to the United Methodist Sunday School, *c.* 1900. The entrance was in Bakers Lane. Before the infants' (now primary) school was built on High Street, the Sunday school building was rented by the Over School Board for infant teaching. The main hall had full stage facilities which were often used for concerts and theatrical performances.

The Salvation Army took over a building from the teetotal 'Blue Ribbon Army' in late Victorian times. They both preached a strict teetotal philosophy, but their band music attracted many people a hundred years ago and they often played outside public houses to get their message to those who needed it. This building was in Weaver Street, near where the Citadel stands today.

This area was once known as Ranter's Row. The chapel at the right stood by a stream known as Ranter's Brook and close by two small streams joined, they were known as The Bride and Groom. Methodists provided chapels in remote areas where the travelling preachers could visit congregations of farm or factory workers who were not able to travel themselves.

No book of Winsford could miss out the Devil. The story invented to explain why St Chad's church was so far from the village was that the Devil stole the church from Delamere Street and dropped it in the fields. In actual fact the new borough was built around 1300 but the people could not take the burial ground with them. However since the development of the Town Fields the church is almost back in the town again.

Six

The Demon Drink

The oldest pub in Winsford was probably the Blue Bell Inn by the gates of St Chad's church, which served refreshments to parishioners, especially if bad weather made them delay returning home after service. Pubs were used for many functions in the past. The George and Dragon was the meeting place for the mayor's grand jury while drunks were tried and fined in the pub without any sense of irony. The mayor's ale tasters tested the quality of each pub in Over before the mayor granted licences to them! Some were quite grand 'Commercial Hotels' which indicated that a commercial traveller could stay there, and more importantly, that his customers could visit him there without fear for their reputations. They offered meals and other facilities, and some still have their stables where horses and carriages could be hired to take customers home. Some had an outdoor licence with a separate entrance. Most were simple beer houses, set up after tax on beer was repealed in 1831, providing basic rooms and selling beer or porter from the cask but not wines or spirits. Many gathered around the bridge and were the town's red light district for men from the barges. After taxation was reintroduced and opening times were restricted during the First World War magistrates were empowered to close pubs if it was felt that there were too many in one area – only half now continue to trade.

Winsford's oldest hostelry is the old Blue Bell, formerly a farm pub which lost its license in 1930, and was later rebuilt after a fire. Until recently it was operated as a tea shop by the parish and visitors could call in during summer afternoons. At the extreme left is the former hearse house where a horse-drawn vehicle was stored to be taken for the coffin when needed.

The oldest building serving as a pub is Knight's Grange, on the site of a farm that belonged to the monks of Vale Royal. It was built in the early seventeenth century as a home for the third son of Lady Mary Cholmondeley, the *Bolde Ladie* of Cheshire, and was formerly moated. The 'barn' (actually a shippon) of 1844 is used for functions – the bricks used cost 9s for a thousand!

The old Market Place was full of pubs, and was notorious also as the haunt of 'good time girls', so respectable women would avoid it after dark. It was close to the places where boats tied up for the night and besides local men there were often sailors with money to spend. In this scene no less than five pubs can be seen; of them only the Red Lion remains unchanged.

The demolition of the 'three pubs in a row' (Ship, Flatman's Cabin and Coach and Horses) with the former Weaver House Stores. It is easy to see how the stores was made up of plank construction and not brick because this was the area most affected by subsidence, but it was a great fire risk. The Red Lion Hotel is on the left.

This was 'the only building in Winsford', as every other was either Wharton or Over! Although a pub called the Red Lion existed in 1721 (when the Weaver was made navigable) the present building is late Victorian timber frame to resist subsidence. Then the ornamental gaslight was the only one left alight all night when Winsford was called 'Dark Town'.

For a time the access to the Dene Estate from High Street was through a cinder track next to the Queen's Arms. It was demolished so that Dene Drive could be extended and a new larger pub was built in 1958. In the 1960s and '70s the new pub was a popular evening venue with its own 'discotheque' added in a room to the side.

Winsford's unique pub name was the Rechabite's Rest on the corner of Dingle Lane. It was said to be named in honour of John Dodd, son of a blacksmith from Darnhall, who was expelled from the strictly teetotal Order of Rechabites for giving his farm labourers their traditional 'harvest ale'. However, the row of cottages nearby was called Rechabite's Terrace. The trees to the left of the pub were called The Drumber, a name now used for a modern street.

There were two Bull's Heads in High Street. This one stood at the end of Factory Street until 1965 and was where the bodies of the people who died in the Cotton Mill fire of 1874 were taken to be identified. Factory Street became Geneva Road shortly afterwards, but no one is really sure why the name change was made, as part of the factory continued in use.

The other Bull's Head was at the corner of Weaver Street. It was replaced by Skellon's shoe shop after 1919 because the license was taken away from the pub as magistrates tried to reduce the numbers of ale houses. The introduction of restricted hours during the First World War and a popular anti-alcohol movement affected the whole country's drinking habits.

The author's grandfather's name is displayed above the door of this pub and records show he was landlord in the 1890s; the lady was his first wife and he married the author's grandmother when she died. The working class nature of the pub's clients can be judged by the fact that it sold porter, which was a thick dark ale drunk by porters and other manual workers as it supposedly made them strong.

The White Swan was known to all as 'Th' Mucky Duck', because its white limestone carved swan collected soot from the smoky atmosphere and turned black. It stood almost opposite the gates of High Street Primary School close to the modern library. Notice the old painted advertisement on the side, such permanent advertising was common in a more stable age.

Seven
Public Buildings

As the town grew in importance there was a need for public buildings which reflected the ideals of a Victorian middle class way of life – away from the ale house. The Golden and Diamond Jubilees (1887 and 1897 respectively) were the ideal occasions to mark with public buildings, although few of the things provided to mark the events actually opened to coincide exactly with them. Public subscriptions were taken and in 1887 there were debates about what was the greatest priority. The options show the concerns of the time, that a swimming bath, recreation grounds or a library should be opened – the Medical Officer of Health's suggestion that a decent abattoir was more important was ignored! In the event, the recreation grounds in Over and Wharton were donated by local land-owners, and were important in an age when most land was considered private and out of bounds. The swimming baths were provided by the Verdins and so the public library was the only option left. The Technical Schools were also provided by the Verdin family. They had owned salt work and barges on the Weaver and were the biggest shareholders in the Salt Union. Over Hall was given to the town after being used by the military during the Second World War and became the council offices until a new purpose-built office block at Wyvern House was opened by Princess Margaret in 1991. Its name is taken from the mythical beasts which hold the Borough shield. Many public buildings were constructed during the overspill era including one of the largest libraries in the county, with centres for old people and youngsters.

The town hall stood next to the bridge on the Wharton side and was a general purpose meeting and function room, not to be confused with municipal town halls which contain the council offices. The ground floor was a row of shops with a meeting and function room above it in which Winsford people first watched moving pictures.

The oldest surviving public buildings are the former Market Hall, which is now St John's School, and the market cross next to it. This structure of around 1840 is totally unique as it contains the 'lock up' – a prison cell – and was originally enclosed within an iron rail to prevent school children climbing on it. Iron rails were removed as part of an ill-conceived war effort.

A police station for the whole town of Winsford was built to replace separate police stations when the county council became responsible for policing. It was built in red terracotta, as were most public buildings, for the very practical reason that soot would not stick to the brick. It had a magistrates' courts upstairs and cells for prisoners which replaced the lock up.

The first public library was erected in 1888 using money raised to celebrate Queen Victoria's Golden Jubilee. It was the town's first publicly owned building and contained a lending library, a reference and reading room along with a room at the back in which adult art classes were held. It was the first step towards making Winsford a respectable place to live.

The Verdin gifts to the town were numerous. The swimming baths were presented in 1887 to mark Queen Victoria's Golden Jubilee. They were housed in a building with a pitch pine frame and besides swimming in brine they offered 'slipper baths' and showers to remove the salt afterwards. A fire in 1918 in the woodwork destroyed them completely.

Swimming fashions have changed considerably since this group posed in knitted one-piece costumes at the turn of the century. The baths were used for many sporting events – as the medals and shield show – and attracted people from as far away as Crewe who travelled along the North Western railway sideline to the town to make use of the baths for exercise.

Winsford opened a lido in Rilshaw Lane in 1935 to allow people to bathe and sunbathe in privacy. The pool was filled with brine which was icy cold and the high walls prevented anyone being offended in an age when it was still not normal to go out without a hat. The tower contained a tank of water for the showers to wash away the salt crystals.

Although viewed around twenty years later, to judge by the women's dresses, this picture of the brine baths shows that the spectators still kept very much covered up. On both sides of the pool were areas to sit with sunshades while at the far end is the diving platform. The fountain on the right had warmer water and was popular among smaller visitors.

When William Henry Verdin moved out of Highfield House to Darnhall Hall it was given to the town to become an infirmary to mark the 1897 Jubilee. Nurses wearing long aprons are shown in this contemporary photograph. The building served for less urgent cases until hospital services were centred at Leighton Hospital near Crewe in the '70s.

The wealthy of Winsford never missed an opportunity of doing good for the community, and it was a principal of Victorian and Edwardian middle class living that you were seen to be serving on the right committees, especially married ladies who were not expected to do any paid work. This record of summer fashions with parasols to shade delicate faces shows the Hospital Committee.

A fire in 1946 raged through the upper floors of the council offices leaving the councillors nowhere to meet. As an emergency measure they moved into the Victorian Over Hall which had been given to the town after being used by the military in the war. The Urban District Council and then Vale Royal Council were to use Over Hall until the 1990s.

The ground floor of the council offices was comparatively undamaged and continued to be used by the Ministry of Pensions as local offices until the '60s. This picture shows the view into Church Street with the Waterman's church on the right and the chimneys of Hamlett's Salt works beyond it. The single gaslight on the gatepost of the church is a charming reminder of past times.

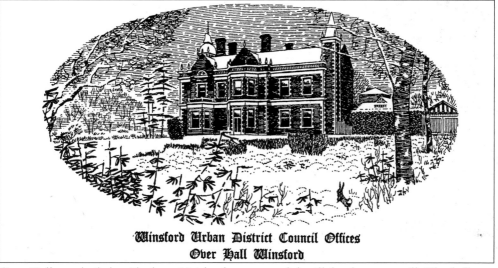

Winsford Urban District Council Offices
Over Hall Winsford

Over Hall was built by Abraham Haigh, the owner of the ill-fated cotton mill. The hall was requisitioned for war work and then given to the town. It was originally intended to be a maternity hospital and rest home in its own park, however, the Urban District Council moved their offices there after the fire, then Vale Royal Council sold the hall and park for building in 1991.

The Drill Hall was built for volunteer soldiers – a Victorian version of 'Dad's Army' – who were first recruited in the mid-nineteenth century when there was a threat of invasion from Napoleon III. By the time of the Boer War they were an active force in Winsford. After the First World War they ceased to exist and the hall became the Palace Cinema and is now a bingo club.

A postcard printed only a few years after the opening of the Brunner Guild Hall. It was promised after the Verdins gave the Technical School to mark Queen Victoria's Diamond Jubilee on Jubilee Day 1897 and opened in 1899 to provide meeting rooms and other facilities away from public houses – serving alcohol there is still not allowed for any function.

Crowds gathered for every occasion in Victorian Winsford and these people eye the camera man with curiosity as he records the opening of the Brunner Guild Hall in 1899. The opening was accompanied by processions including one of decorated bicycles, a speciality of old Winsford which vanished with coming of the motor car.

During the 1890s Winsford developed an impressive range of civic building on the High Street away from subsidence. This view was posted in 1904, the Board School (run by the School Board) was redesigned shortly afterwards when the headmaster's house in the centre of the picture was converted into more classroom space and the front was altered.

New Council Offices at Wyvern House opened in 1991. Although this was to bring services together under one roof for the first time, the Cold War conditions at the time also required a full scale nuclear bunker in which officials could shelter in case of nuclear war and emerge to organize things afterwards. The chief executive is seen discussing the opening. The fall of Communism and the end of the Cold War overtook the building project and it was obsolete by the time it was ready.

There had been no Labour Party Club in Winsford before the overspill development, when a large social club with dance floor and stage was built next to the Queen's Hotel. However, financial problems caused it to close and it became a nightclub which in turn closed to be replaced by late night music clubs near the river. A supermarket now occupies the site.

Eight
School Days

Over and Wharton were administered as separate towns until 1895, and until 1901 they each had their own Local Boards of Education responsible for building and maintaining schools from 1870. They were mainly elementary schools at which children were educated from five until thirteen. Before Education was made compulsory there had been a variety of schools including a charity school in the old Market Hall at Over from the 1840s which became the Church School of St John's parish. The Navigation School for St Chad's parish in Weaver Street was provided for the families of boat people and other poor children who were taught in one large room by a single teacher. At Meadow Bank Herman Falk provided his own school for the families of workers employed by him. Education became the responsibility of the county council in 1902. After the Second World War the school leaving age was raised to fifteen and a new two-tier system of education was introduced with the former Board Schools in Over and Wharton becoming secondary moderns and a grammar school offering a more academic education to those who passed the 11-plus exams in the former Technical Schools. In the 1960s, as the town developed, the county policy was to segregate the sexes and a new school intended for girls only was built in Grange Lane. When co-educational comprehensive education was introduced the Verdin was the biggest such school in the country until Woodford Lodge was opened to take half the pupils in 1971. At that time two or three new schools a year opened to provide education for the new estates as half of the people who moved to Winsford were under school leaving age.

The Weaver Navigation provided three churches with their church schools in Runcorn, Northwich and Winsford where children of people living on the boats could attend. The school was in Weaver Street and as the head was Mr Dunn, it was called 'Dun's (pronounced Dunce) School'. It was replaced by the school in Gladstone Street in 1909.

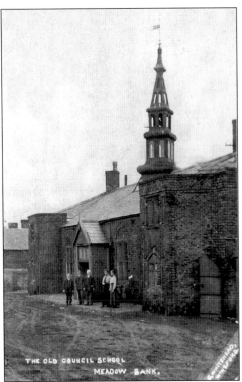

When the education acts prevented the employment of children in the salt works, Herman Falk was afraid that many of his employees would leave the houses he provided for them at Meadow Bank to move nearer the schools. To prevent this a remarkable school was built using Bass, the material which was left in the hearths under the salt pans.

Things never turn out as we expect them to be! This architect's drawing of the Verdin Technical Schools shows chickens in the road outside – today it is a busy dual carriageway with zebra crossings and traffic lights close to the shopping centre. It became the Verdin Grammar School but is now the town's adult education centre.

This group of girls from Wharton School are typical of the late Victorian era. As they grew older, the more able ones were chosen as 'pupil teachers' who were taught by the teacher and then spent some of the day teaching basic literacy and numeracy to the younger ones. Only if the family could provide enough finance could they then train as certified teachers.

By way of contrast this is the author's class at High Street Primary School in the 1950s. All the boys had short trousers and wore sandals. They started school at three years old in 1950 in special nursery classes where the children had an afternoon nap on camp beds. As there was a shortage of male workers, because of National Service, this allowed mothers to work in their place.

There was a two-tier education system between the wars; there were elementary (Board or Church) schools for everyone and brighter pupils could pass a scholarship to the Technical Schools. Passing the Verdin scholarship was only one obstacle, parents had to be able to afford a full uniform and slips for 'drill', as shown here, or their children could not go.

Empire Day (24 May and Queen Victoria's birthday) was marked by children in the imagined costume of different countries or simply draped in flags. Each child would say a poem or sing a song about the country that they represented. Note that Africans, Asians and West Indians are all missing. On 29 May an oak leaf for Royal Oak Day was worn.

The Government introduced free school milk after the Second World War and every child had a third of a pint each morning. These pupils at Wharton School are all enjoying their morning drink from bottles which had wide tops for cardboard stoppers. The wooden desks with cast iron frames and tip up seats were standard from Victorian times until the 1960s, as were ink wells.

The Grange School (now Verdin) was intended to be a girls only Secondary Modern School when it was built and it featured two large domestic science rooms. Most girls are making cakes while ironing is undertaken on the left. The Secondary Moderns provided practical education and for many girls in the 1960s preparing to run an efficient home was still their main interest.

Woodford Lodge was the first school to be built especially for the county's new policy of co-educational comprehensive education and was set in a greenfields site on the edge of town. Hebden Green School for children with special needs is nearing completion in this 1974 photograph while the 'White Cliffs of Over' on the Mount Pleasant estate are conspicuous.

Nine
Leisure

In Edwardian times a row on the river was a happy time and people from surrounding towns would come along the railway branch lines into the stations near the Flash. The town is still a centre for sailing and caravans. The first cinema films were shown in the rickety timber town hall which was owned by a private company and stood near the bridge. In the 1950s Winsford had the Magnet and Palace Cinemas. The Palace was created out of the Drill Hall where the volunteer soldiers – known as the Buttermilk army because they drank that in preference to beer – used to meet before the First World War. It is now a bingo hall. Roller skating was a popular pastime in the inter-war period with a special rink by the old post office. During the 1950s and 1960s the Strand Ballroom was the place to meet for dancing and if you needed to learn there were classes at 'Dodd's' in a former factory on Station Road. In Edwardian times leisure pursuits were more sedate and a tea party held at the Sunday school or a magic lantern show depicting the evils of drink were more likely. Sunday schools provided all sorts of entertainment ranging from pantomimes and bazaars to raising money for outings and tea parties to special 'Sunday School Treats' or coach trips to the seaside. Later they provided discos, but only for regular Sunday scholars! The Civic Hall was designed for 1,000 disco dancers at a time when big groups would still play in places like Winsford and The Kinks played at the opening night. Some dances there lasted all night! From the 1960s pubs catered for young people with juke boxes and 'discos'. The advent of television in more comfortable homes, along with the ability to travel by car has resulted in an age where the audience has often been so disappointingly small that local events have been either cancelled or run at a considerable loss.

Parades and processions have always been a part of Winsford's history. This picture has been published both as the soldiers leaving *and* returning from the Boer War. On the back of the original are the words 'Over Silver Band, May'. Just what the parade was cannot be verified but we can see they are passing the Wesleyan Methodist church and police station.

Like the Duke of York's soldiers – those that go up the hill must also come down. It is uncertain if these are volunteers leaving for the Boer War or a later group, perhaps at the time of the First World War. Several policemen lead the way but there is nothing in the dress of the onlookers to give a clue to the date as they pass the old police station on High Street.

More marching, this was between the wars, apparently for Civic Sunday. Of special interest is the background with the Central Primitive Methodist chapel built over the Sunday school which was at ground level (left). Hartley's sewing factory was above the shops (centre) and there is a barber's pole where George Dodd later cut hair.

Another civic parade is nearing St Chad's church; as there is only one mace bearer this must have been before 1910 when the second mace was given to the town by Sir John Brunner. John Henry Cooke is in his robes and wig as Recorder of the Ancient Borough of Over, an office which was revived for a few years in the 1890s. Note how narrow the road is!

'Old soldiers never die', they say, and in Winsford they carried on parading. Here with banners flying, the ex-service men leave the Royal British Legion Club (visible right) in Siddorn Street to march to the war memorial, which was by the primary school playground on High Street, 1952. The club became a Kingdom Hall of the Jehovah's Witnesses.

The Over May festival of 1905. This was held on the field behind the Guild Hall where the extension to the grammar school (now Verdin Exchange) was built. The festivities seem to have ended around the time of the First World War, but a few of the rides from Knutsford Royal May Day fair would always set up in Winsford for a few days the following week.

Another Edwardian May Queen with her retinue, each one with a massive ribbon tied around the head as it was considered vulgar to go out without the head covered. Edwardian women's hats were enormous things with wide brims to keep the sun off their faces as a sun tan was also considered to be 'common'. The munitions work of the First World War changed all that!

Recruits were wanted for the army according to the poster – probably for the First World War. This group of costumed characters with the May Queen are full of patriotic feeling too, note the row of little 'jack tars' on the left and beefeaters at the back. Little John Henry Cooke, the town clerk, is there too, keeping everyone in order as usual.

There were almost as many people on the May Festival Committee as there were actually taking part! Here they assembled in huge hats, on the lawns at Over Hall to be recorded for their part as middle class wives of the wealthy Winsfordians. After the First World War the middle class wives did not have such spare time on their hands and a carnival was organized by a less visible working class.

This horse-drawn parade has been included to show how crowds would gather for want of any other entertainment. They are pictured outside the George and Dragon, Delamere Street. It is interesting to note that the working class widows wear smaller bonnets and a shawl, not the big showy hats of the middle class, while the men all wear flat caps.

Political correctness had not been thought of when this group of men posed as the 'Winsford Nigger Minstrels'. Music from black America was only just becoming known as something new and exciting around 1900. The boys all wear wigs to make them look more 'Negro' and only their conductor has a white face – not one shred of offence was ever intended then.

Most people could not afford to leave the town for days out, but railway branch lines could bring visitors close to the riverside on a summer's afternoon. As no man is without his straw boater that suggests this must be the 1920s when the Prince of Wales made such headgear popular. Pleasure boats are on the Bottom Flash, only a few hundred yards from the salt works!

The 1930s was the first time in history that women actually tried to get a sun tan as it showed that they could afford to go on holiday. If you could not afford a holiday you went to the Flashes. The most astonishing thing in this picture of sunbathers to modern eyes is the Filter Beds which processed Winsford's sewage, shown as two square pools, just above their heads.

In 1935 Winsford marked the Diamond Jubilee of King George V with street parties. At this party in Princess Street tea is being served at tables set out down the middle of the road. The decorations won the prize for the best in Winsford; one elderly gentleman, recalling the event, told how he stayed up all night painting the kerb stones in red, white and blue!

This group of fancy dress characters is also pictured in Princess Street, two years later, either for the Coronation of George VI or the first carnival. Among the people in costume is a pair wearing paper mâché heads to look like a giant and his wife. To give an idea of inflation the first prize for best dressed street was £5 and the best dressed house in town received £1!

Unemployment has always been a problem in industrial towns and in the 1930s the closure of so many salt works left many men out of work. A social centre to provide assistance for them and their families was opened and in this picture the children are shown wearing the special frocks that had been made for them to wear on Coronation Day in 1937.

Youths hanging round on street corners was a problem 100 years ago as much as it is today. This pair were recorded near the steps on Wharton Hill with a bottle – whether containing beer or lemonade is not known. Notice the cobble stone path and iron rails, as well as the gas light – all evidence of a vanished way of life in 'Dark Town'.

In 1953 Winsford celebrated the Coronation after years of war and then rationing; a new Queen was to be crowned. The flags were flying again and Dierden Street was decorated. A brass plaque on the former school records the contribution made by the street community in a parade of 1945 to mark the victory. There are many such records of great community involvement in past events of this nature.

There were still stone setts (not cobbles) in Dean Street in 1953 and the flags were flying. Dean Street was one of those developed during the 1870s which housed men who worked in Hamlet's Brick Works. Other names in the area are 'Dene' after the Dene Brook, so it seems probable that Dean Street should also have been 'Dene', but no one checked the spelling.

During the swinging '60s there were many activities for young people. Serving the needs of the 18-30 year olds was the 18 Plus Group. They are pictured here at an evening bonfire party on Little Budworth Common, intent on a bit of barbecuing by the looks of things. The group arranged many social functions during the year; locally and throughout the region.

'Don't loose your head, join 18 Plus' was the theme of this lorry pictured in Nixon Drive, before the carnival procession moved off. The carnival started in 1937 to raise funds for the Albert Infirmary and was organised by the Working Men's Charity Committee; although by the '70s the only serving man was the chairman! The carnival is still a great spectacle each summer.

Ghoulish goings on at an 18 Plus party to mark Halloween in the late '60s. This was held in the room at the George and Dragon where the old time mayors of Over held their courts. Among those who were attracted to the town were a large number of newly qualified young people starting on professional careers – 18 Plus created social contacts for them.

In 1969 a movement to work an hour a week for nothing to help British economy fight in the world market gripped Britain. 'I'm Backing Britain' was the slogan on everyone's lips when this group of Committee members organised an 'I'm Backing Britain' evening; dressed in red white and blue they served up traditional British food at a party in the George and Dragon.

114

Ten
The Changing Face

An idea of producing a 'Then and Now' book of photographs, comparing past scenes with the modern equivalent, was initially suggested to the author. In Winsford the scenes in most cases have changed out of all recognition, as the following series of photographs show. The middle of the town, by the bridge, was known as 'The Bottom of Winsford' because you came down a hill in any direction to get to it, unless you came down the river which was lined by salt works. The shops were mainly half-timbered like those in Northwich. The only building to survive is the old post office, now painted cream and selling fish and chips. Many of the buildings were of plank construction because the area was likely to collapses due to salt subsidence – today they would be an intolerable fire hazard. They had to go, to be replaced by new shops on safer land (according to geologists) part way up High Street. Today the old centre is marked by a small wood on a traffic island surrounded by the busy one-way traffic system. Old Winsford took over a century to evolve but was destroyed in a decade of 'redevelopment'. It is nostalgic to look back at a former age, but few would exchange modern comforts to go back to an age of gas lights and horse-drawn traffic, smoke and subsidence.

Winsford in late Victorian times was called 'the vilest hole' and this picture tells it all. Filthy roads with no proper surface covered with horse muck and mud – and yet the group of men standing in the middle of the road seem oblivious. On the right is a salt pan shed and beyond are the 'seven sisters' chimneys of Hamlett's Salt Work. It was justly 'Dark Town'.

The same view in the 1950s. The salt works chimneys are still there but not for much longer. The Post Office and Woolworth's have brought more substantial buildings to the town centre and there is also a concrete bus shelter. This was the main shopping centre at that date but within another decade practically everything you see here would be gone.

The High Street, seen just after the First World War when people could stand in the middle of the road unconcerned, as a single horse-drawn cart is the only traffic. It shows what was the old commercial centre of the town in the lower part of the High Street in an age of gas lights. Just about everything seen here was demolished in the 1960s and '70s because it was regarded as old-fashioned.

In the 1870s two branch lines were built to bring the railways to the back of the salt works which lined the Weaver. Over, Wharton and Winsford Station served the Cheshire Lines with links to Chester and Manchester with this station close to where the K Club (formerly the Vale Royal pub) is now. You could go to Northwich, Chester or Manchester by train.

The London North Western Railway built a branch line to serve salt works on the east of the river with a timber station opposite the North Western pub. Banks of coal for the engine are on the right. After the 'Big Freeze' in 1963, when lorries queued daily on Wharton Hill for the salt mine, rock salt was stored in a depot here. Wharton Park Way now uses this route.

Originally there were plans for a ring road around Winsford, but only the western portion was completed. Instead half of the old High Street was demolished to create a dual carriageway. This shows, in 1977, where houses and shops have been demolished. The police station is on the right with the terraced houses and 'backs' exposed on the left.

An aerial view at the same time shows the Waterman's church, by then unused, in the bottom right corner and the new road system being constructed with two bridges and a one-way system. The earth from the cuttings was piled in a mound in the centre and planted as a wood. Before this there were traffic jams every morning and evening.

The town pulled out all the stops to welcome new industry to the town and here the chairman of the council and the seneschals march to the opening ceremony of a new project on the industrial estate. Many of the factories offered as many jobs for women as men and a crowd of women watch during their lunch break from the factory.

Much has changed since the first industrial estate was built. The largest factory was for ICL who made mainframe computers as big as a wardrobe, however the introduction of desk top technology rendered the whole factory out of date overnight. Similar changes in other factories and the loss of the town's development area status put many workers out of a job in the '70s.

This records, in 1965, the demolition of one of the landmarks of old Winsford, a huge blue industrial brick retaining wall by the cutting, which took Wharton Road to the bridge. The cutting was made deeper and wider. Weaver Street is in the background.

This scene was recorded between the wars from slightly to the north of the previous one, salt works chimneys and a host of industrial activity is evident while to the left the old High Street is the bustling centre of a busy small town. Redevelopment planned away almost the whole of this activity in an attempt to create a new town – that now looks 'dated'.

The original idea of overspill development was to provide houses around existing facilities in towns with their own characters. The developers lost sight of that ideal in the '70s and erased a busy town centre completely. This served to further the split of the town into two halves. High Street was pictured in the 1930s with bikes, bus and pedestrians.

The view from Wharton in this old postcard shows a bustling Victorian town, on the left the town hall can be seen with its distinctive tower. Developed during the nineteenth century without any form of planning its nickname, 'Dark Town', did not just relate to the lack of light, but to the unchristian ways of many of the salt workers and their families.

These two views were taken from roughly the same point and around the same time, about sixty years ago. This one shows the pretty Bottom Flash with its pleasure boats. The name Cheshire broads was used in advertising between the wars – but was dropped when the American version of the word 'broad' started to be applied to courting couples there!

The not so attractive aspect of old Winsford is illustrated in this view with the old Town Bridge in the distance. Looking out from where the newer bridge is now, the view shows the old Co-op warehouse in Weaver Street. Goods for the shops were imported by river and unloaded under cover by hoists in the overhanging section.

Winsford does not strike people as a holiday destination, but since Victorian times visitors have come to the side of the Flashes to camp and caravan. Many of the vehicles stationed along the river are permanent homes, while others are used regularly at weekends and holidays. In pre-war days many were substandard, but today the sites have all modern facilities.

It is difficult to relate this scene to the present day, as all that survives is the bridge you can see in the distance. This area is now a woodland, between the two bridges, in the middle of the one-way system which was developed in the 1970s to ease traffic flow on a bridge designed for horses and carts and not for hundreds of cars every hour. Salt barges can be seen behind the old Town Hall.

Memories of early motoring days are evoked by this picture of the post office opposite the High Street Schools. A motorist could, at one time, park by the side of the main road to be filled up with petrol by the sub post master! This narrow road was the main thoroughfare through the town until the 1970s carrying coaches and heavy lorries bound for North Wales.

The days when milk came direct from the farm are recalled in this picture of a milk float at Knight's Grange. The telephone number was easy to remember – just 108. The milking parlour and hay store in the background were converted into changing rooms and a function room mistakenly named 'The Barn' when the farm became a pub at the centre of a sports ground.

Milk is also being delivered in this earlier picture of Delamere Street. This time, before the First World War, it is from metal churns, carried by horse-drawn cart, that the housewife's jug is filled at the door. It was a great age for bikes and no one cared which side of the road you were on as there were no cars. Notice the bike shop on the left.

Farms were on the main roads in old Winsford, this one still stands next to St John's school although the barn is almost derelict. Much farm land was taken over in the redevelopment and farmers were among those most against overspill, as they saw it would take away their farm land and spoil the countryside.

This is claimed to be the oldest photograph of Winsford United Football Club. They wear long 'shorts' held up by leather belts, leather boots with four studs and rolled up shirt sleeves – attire which would almost be suitable for going to work. There is no information about which cup is on show nor where and when the photograph was taken.

The North Western (now Top House) was named as it was the place to wait for trains on the North Western railway which had a station opposite. When the Barton Stadium was given to the town for its football team, matches on Good Friday were forbidden and, as Reginald Barton (the donor) was not a drinker, any alcohol had to be consumed here and not taken to the field.

The river was the reason for Winsford developing, and in 1837 Robert Stephenson, of Rocket fame, built the railway past the town. It crossed the river on this viaduct designed by Joseph Locke, who later built the first houses in Crewe. This steam train is crossing the viaduct on its way from Glasgow to London.

Had it not been for the salt trade Over would be a pretty village and Wharton a sleepy hamlet. The works brought industry, prosperity, smoke and grime. These outside pans were used to make very coarse salt by slowly simmering to create large crystals. Along with the salt works a whole way of life in Winsford vanished in the twentieth century.

Old Winsford was vanishing at the time the old High Street was pictured in the 1970s. Some shops have already been demolished and those on the south of the road are boarded up and empty, awaiting development. Behind is the gas tower, a landmark which may soon be demolished as well. This once busy street is now nothing more than a piece of disused road.

Epilogue

Over 1,000 people toiled in the salt works of Victorian Winsford, but by the 1950s practically all those jobs had gone. Winsford had to be reborn, but was it for the better? In this book old and not so old photographs have been arranged to record this change. We see the Winsford that the former generations saw as they went about their lives, where they worked, where they lived, where they shopped, how they spent their leisure time and where they worshipped. For most who look at these photographs for the first time it will be a strange place that they see. Many who now live in Winsford will find the old place as curious as looking at pictures of ancient Rome or Egypt and, like those past empires, the Empire of Queen Victoria is now part of the National Curriculum. Winsford was known as 'Dark Town', not only because the smoke hid the sunlight, but to many it seemed as unchristian and uncivilised as 'Darkest Africa'.

Winsford was growing anew when Queen Victoria came to the throne; but when Elizabeth II was crowned it was in serious decline. Jobs being lost when the salt industry was modernized. Despite local opposition to the idea of overspill at first, many young families, almost half of them under school leaving age, came to live in bright new homes to make a new life and a new town. Winsford was rebuilt, now three times the size it was when the old Queen died. This is not a book of pretty pictures – a book of Winsford could never be that for Winsford was a Victorian industrial town – it is a portrait of a place which has changed beyond belief.

The opportunity has been taken to attempt to tell the social and economic history of the town in pictures, not in dates and events, but by showing the way that people lived in this Cheshire town during the nineteenth and twentieth centuries and some of the individuals who lived there. In 1949 F.H. Crosley wrote 'Winsford never had any pretensions to beauty; it has the attributes of a town given over to the more grimy forms of trade. Rows of belching chimneys, a soot-laden atmosphere, with a lack of dignified substantial buildings.' How much has changed?